CAPTIVE

Faith, Survival, and the Cost of Silence

By Aliya Fitz El

“Even when they caged my body, they could not cage my spirit.”

CAPTIVE

Faith, Survival, and the Cost of Silence

By Aliya Fitz El

This book is a memoir based on the author's lived experiences and recollection of events. Certain names or identifying details may be changed where appropriate to protect privacy.

ISBN: 979-8-9954951-0-9

Library of Congress Control Number: 2026907642

Published by

Divine Essence Healing Ministry

Rocky Mount, North Carolina

Printed in the united states of America

I. Dedication

I dedicate this to the me who was silenced.

This is for the me that was scared with no support.

This is for the me who held God's hand as He covered me from the devils in cammies.

This is dedicated to anyone who has ever been silenced or carried shame.

Love Community. Love thyself.

II. Trigger Warning & Grounding Exercise

Trigger Warning

This book contains first-hand accounts of military sexual trauma (MST), institutional abuse, medical neglect, confinement, and psychological harm. Some passages may be activating for survivors of trauma.

Please read at your own pace. You are encouraged to pause, skip sections, or step away whenever needed.

You are not weak for needing care.
Your body is responding to remembered harm.

Before continuing, you may wish to use the grounding exercise below.

Grounding & Breathing Exercise

(For Moments of Distress)

If at any point while reading you feel overwhelmed, anxious, disconnected, or emotionally flooded, stop here and do the following exercise. This is not about forcing calm—it is about bringing your body back into the present moment.

Step 1: Orient

- Place your feet flat on the ground.
- If possible, sit upright and rest your hands on your thighs.
- Look around and quietly name 5 things you can see.
- Step 2: Regulated Breathing (4–6 Pattern)
- Inhale slowly through your nose for 4 seconds.
- Hold gently for 2 seconds.
- Exhale slowly through your mouth for 6 seconds.

- Repeat this cycle 5 times.

(Longer exhales signal safety to the nervous system.)

Step 3: Body Check

- Notice where your body is tense.
- Without judgment, say quietly: *"I am safe right now."*
- If helpful, place one hand on your chest or stomach.

Step 4: Choice

- Decide whether to continue reading, take a break, or stop for now.
- All choices are valid.

This book will still be here when you are ready.

Prologue

There are stories people refuse to believe—until the truth claws its way into the light. Mine is one of them. Not because it is rare, but because it is all too common. Hidden. Buried. Silenced.

I wore the uniform with pride. I bled for a country that never once bled for me. I was a Marine—trained, tested, and trusted. Until I wasn't.

Until I was caged.

This is not just my story. It is a cry for justice, a voice for those who were silenced in the shadows of barracks and behind locked doors. It is the voice of every woman, every man, every Marine who raised their right hand and said, "I will serve," only to find themselves betrayed by the very system that swore to protect them.

This is for the survivors. This is for the truth. This is Captive.

Reader Invitation

Before you continue reading, I ask something simple of you.

Read this story with honesty.

The experiences described in these pages are not comfortable. They are not meant to be sensational or dramatic. They are the reality of what can happen when power is misused and silence is expected.

For many years I carried these memories quietly. Like many survivors, I believed that survival meant moving forward without speaking about what happened. But silence does not erase truth. It only hides it.

This book exists so that truth can stand in the light.

As you read, remember that this story is not mine alone. Across the military and across institutions, there are many service members who have endured harm in silence. Many continue to serve while carrying experiences they have never been allowed to name publicly.

If you are a survivor reading this, know that you are not alone.

If you are someone who has never experienced this kind of harm, I ask that you read with empathy and with the understanding that survival often looks quieter than people expect.

This book is not written to seek revenge. It is written to bear witness.

Truth matters. Accountability matters. And the voices of survivors deserve to exist without fear or dismissal.

Thank you for reading with an open mind and a steady heart.

— Aliya Fitz El

CHAPTER 1

Called to Serve

I believed service meant protection. Not in an abstract way. In a practical one. I believed that if you followed the rules, respected authority, and did what was asked of you, there was a structure in place that would keep you safe. That belief didn't come from naivety. It came from being raised to trust systems that promised order.

At nineteen, I wanted direction. Purpose. A place where effort mattered and sacrifice meant something. I wanted to belong to something larger than myself — something that claimed honor as its foundation.

When I raised my right hand, the room felt still. The words were formal, rehearsed, older than me. I repeated them carefully, aware that this moment would change the trajectory of my life. I didn't feel fear. I felt resolved.

I didn't yet understand that belief itself can be a vulnerability.

The paperwork began almost immediately. Forms slid across desks. Instructions were given quickly, without pause for questions. I signed where I was told to sign. Initialed where I was told to initial. Each mark felt ceremonial, like proof that I was moving forward.

No one asked how young I was.
No one asked what I understood consent to mean.

The system didn't need to ask. My willingness was assumed.

I walked out of that room proud, unaware that I had just agreed to give more than I could yet comprehend.

CHAPTER 2

Becoming Government Property

Belonging quickly became documentation. My body was measured and approved. Height. Weight. Vision. Blood pressure. Everything that could be quantified was logged. What couldn't be measured was ignored. The process was efficient, almost comforting in its precision.

There was no space to hesitate. Helps were posted on the walls, but the pace made it clear that falling behind was not an option. Confusion was treated as personal failure, not a signal to slow down.

I learned early that compliance was rewarded with quiet approval. Questions created friction.

My marriage was recorded. Emergency contacts listed. Beneficiaries named. Entire relationships reduced to boxes on a page. I remember feeling a strange mix of security and exposure — as if my life had been neatly organized, but no longer fully mine.

At nineteen, I didn't think of this as ownership. I thought of it as structure.

Looking back, I see how thoroughly my identity was absorbed into the system. Once documented, I was manageable. Once manageable, I was replaceable.

I didn't resist. I didn't question. I believed I was doing what was required to succeed.

I didn't yet know that the same paperwork that organizes you can later be used to erase you.

CHAPTER 3

Cherry Point

Arrival has a sound. Boots on concrete. Doors opening and closing. Voices echoing down long hallways where everything smells faintly of cleaning solution and old air. Cherry Point announced itself as functional, not welcoming.

Orders brought me there, cleanly typed and official. On paper, it was a simple transition. In reality, it was the first place where I felt truly alone inside the system.

Housing came with rules that extended beyond walls. Inspections were frequent. Privacy was conditional. Even when I was off duty, I was never entirely off watch. I learned to keep things in order, not just for cleanliness, but to avoid attention.

Medical appointments continued. Dental work. Routine check-ins. Everything appeared normal. Everything was documented. And still, I began to feel a quiet alertness settle into my body. Not fear — not yet — but awareness. A sense that I needed to pay attention to tone as much as instruction. To timing as much as location.

I noticed how often I was told to wait. How often instructions were vague. How easily I could end up alone in places that felt too enclosed for comfort.

No one told me I was unsafe.

But no one made sure I was safe either.

CHAPTER 4

The First Shift

Something changed before I had words for it. At first, it was subtle — an awareness that arrived before understanding. A tightening in my chest when footsteps slowed behind me. A hesitation before opening doors that had never made me pause before. I started noticing how often I was alone when I hadn't planned to be.

Cherry Point still looked the same on the outside. Same buildings. Same routines. Same rules posted on walls as if safety could be guaranteed by signage alone. But my body had begun to register a difference.

I remember standing in a hallway one afternoon, the air thick with disinfectant and stale coffee, waiting for instructions that were never clear. The longer I stood there, the quieter it became. Conversations faded. Doors closed. I became aware of how few witnesses there were to anything that happened beyond those walls.

No one had touched me.
No one had threatened me.

Not yet.

And still, something in me understood that I was being watched — not in a protective way, but in a way that made my movements feel smaller. Measured. A door closed behind me — not slammed, just shut with intention. A pause that lasted too long. A voice that filled the room while leaving no space for mine.

I focused on details that didn't matter. The clock. The hum of the lights. The way my body went still without my permission. Later, paperwork would describe those interactions as routine. Nothing about them felt routine to me.

CHAPTER 5

The Body Learns First

Before my mind could name what was happening, my body had already adjusted. Sleep became lighter. Sounds registered faster. I began choosing routes based on visibility rather than convenience. I learned where to stand so I wasn't boxed in. Where to sit so I could see the door.

None of this was conscious at first. It felt instinctive — automatic. As if my body had started gathering information I hadn't yet processed. Medical check-ins continued, unchanged in tone. Questions were asked. Answers were recorded. Everything appeared normal. No one asked why my shoulders were always tense or why my breathing shortened in certain spaces.

I didn't offer explanations. I didn't know how.

I remember moments where time seemed to stretch — seconds thickening as voices lowered, as proximity shifted just enough to register. I learned to keep my expression neutral. To respond quickly. To avoid giving anything that could be misread.

Freezing didn't feel dramatic. It felt practical.

Later, I would hear questions framed as curiosity: *Why didn't you speak up? Why didn't you leave?* Those questions assume that safety was available. My body knew otherwise.

It learned first — what my mind would take much longer to accept — that survival sometimes looks like stillness, and silence can be a strategy rather than a choice.

CHAPTER 6

Rooms Without Witnesses

There are places where nothing is officially supposed to happen. Rooms that exist for paperwork, briefings, routine conversations. Spaces that look neutral on the surface — desks, chairs, fluorescent lights humming overhead. Doors meant to open and close without consequence.

I learned quickly which rooms felt different.

They weren't marked. There were no signs warning me to be careful. But my body recognized them the moment I stepped inside. The air felt heavier. The silence pressed in. The door always seemed farther away once it closed.

Sometimes I was told to wait. Sometimes to sit. Sometimes instructions were delivered casually, as if nothing out of the ordinary was occurring. The tone suggested familiarity, expectation — as though my presence there was assumed.

I remember the way voices changed in those rooms. Lower. Slower. As if time itself had shifted. Questions were asked that didn't quite feel like questions. Statements delivered that left no space for response.

I learned to answer carefully. Briefly. I learned that too much explanation could be used against me, but silence could be interpreted as defiance. Every interaction felt like a calculation I hadn't been taught how to solve.

The door mattered.

Whether it stayed open or closed changed everything. An open door meant witnesses — even imagined ones. A closed door meant uncertainty. I became acutely aware of the sound it made when it shut. Not loud enough to draw attention. Just firm enough to signal finality.

I don't remember every word that was said in those rooms. What stayed with me was the way my body reacted — how my shoulders tightened, how my breathing shortened, how my focus narrowed to the smallest details in front of me.

I started noticing patterns. How often these conversations happened when no one else was nearby. How frequently I was isolated under the guise of routine tasks. How easily authority could turn ordinary spaces into places of control.

No one told me I could refuse to enter those rooms.

And even if they had, I'm not sure refusal would have felt possible. I was nineteen, conditioned to comply, trained to interpret discomfort as weakness rather than warning.

Later, I would be asked why I didn't name these moments more clearly. Why didn't I document them? Why didn't I say something sooner? But rooms without witnesses are designed for exactly that purpose — to leave no record beyond the one the institution chooses to keep.

What happened in those spaces didn't need to be dramatic to be damaging. It only needed to be repeated. Quietly. Consistently. Without interruption. By the time I understood what was happening, the pattern had already taken hold.

And the system would soon give it a different name.

CHAPTER 7

The Charge

The first sign that something was wrong wasn't the accusation. It was the silence. Conversations stopped when I entered rooms. Instructions that had once come freely were suddenly delivered through others or not at all. I was told to wait — and then told nothing. Days passed in a fog of uncertainty where my presence felt tolerated rather than acknowledged.

No one explained what was happening.
No one asked for my side of anything.

I remember being called in and handed paperwork without preamble. No buildup. No warning. Just pages placed in front of me, the tone already shifted from conversational to procedural. The language was clean. Clinical. Final. Dates. Allegations. Locations.

I read the words more than once, certain I had misunderstood them. The accusations did not align with my reality, yet they were written with a confidence that suggested the conclusion had already been reached.

My age did not appear anywhere on those pages.
Neither did context.
Neither did fear.

I remember the room vividly — the hard chair, the scuffed floor, the way the air felt too still. I remember how my hands went numb as I tried to hold the papers steady enough to read. How my mouth went dry even though no one was asking me questions.

I wasn't being investigated.
I was being processed.

When I tried to speak, I was told to listen. When I asked for clarification, I was told the process would explain itself. The words *routine* and *procedure* were repeated like reassurance, as if repetition alone could make them true. What struck me most was how little emotion accompanied the moment. There was no anger. No urgency. Just efficiency. That efficiency was terrifying.

I realized then that whatever had happened in those rooms without witnesses had already been translated into something else — something portable. Something that could move through channels without me. Paper travels faster than truth.

I was nineteen years old and suddenly aware that my future was being decided in places I could not enter, by people who did not know me beyond what was written in front of them. I remember thinking, *If this is wrong, someone will correct it.* That belief did not last long.

Each step that followed assumed the charge was valid. Meetings were scheduled around it. Decisions referenced it. My role shifted from participant to subject. I wasn't asked what had happened. I was told what would happen next.

By the time I left that room, the story of me had already been rewritten. Not with facts, but with assertions. Not with care, but with certainty.

The charge did not just accuse me of something.

It gave the system permission to stop seeing me as a person.

CHAPTER 8

Consent Under Command

They told me I had rights. That was the word they used — *rights* — delivered in the same tone used for instructions and schedules, as if the meaning were self-evident. Papers were placed in front of me again, stacked neatly, already arranged in the order they expected me to read them.

I was told this was standard.
I was told this was routine.
I was told this was for my benefit.

The explanation came quickly. Too quickly. Sentences blurred together, legal language folded into itself, and every option was presented as if it carried equal weight. I was nineteen years old, sitting across from authority, trying to process consequences that stretched far beyond that room. I remember nodding more than speaking.

Questions felt risky. Each pause carried the implication that I was making things more difficult than they needed to be. I had already learned that cooperation was interpreted as maturity, while hesitation was framed as attitude. The choices were laid out, but none of them felt real.

I could request this.
I could decline that.
I could sign.
I could wait.

What they did not say — what did not need to be said — was how refusal would be received. The room made that clear. The posture. The silence after certain questions. The subtle shift in tone when I tried to slow the process down.

Consent under command does not feel like consent.
It feels like calculation.

I scanned the pages, trying to understand what each signature would mean later — not just tomorrow, but months from now, years from now. There was no time offered to absorb that weight. The process moved forward regardless of my pace.

I remember the pen in my hand. Heavier than it should have been. I remember thinking that once ink touched paper, something permanent would be set in motion. When I signed, it wasn't because I agreed with what was happening.

It was because resistance did not feel survivable.

They thanked me for my cooperation. That word landed strangely. As if I had participated willingly rather than navigated pressure as best I could. As if my compliance validated the process.

Later, those signatures would be cited as proof that everything had been fair. That I had been informed. That I had chosen. What the record would not capture was the reality of that moment — the imbalance, the urgency, the unspoken consequences that shaped every decision.

The illusion of choice is one of the system's most effective tools. Once consent is recorded, context disappears. By the time I stood up to leave, the path ahead had narrowed. The system was no longer deciding *whether* something would happen.

It was deciding *how*.

CHAPTER 9

Confinement

Confinement doesn't announce itself. There is no dramatic moment where everything changes at once. It arrives quietly, through restriction. Through waiting. Through being told where to stand and when to sit, and realizing that none of those decisions belong to you anymore.

I was given instructions without explanation. Where to go. What time to be there. What not to do. The language was precise, stripped of emotion, as if what was happening to me were a logistical adjustment rather than a rupture.

Time became distorted almost immediately.

Hours stretched in ways that felt unnatural. Minutes slowed, then vanished. I waited in rooms that were too cold or too quiet, rooms with chairs bolted to the floor and walls that offered nothing to look at except scuff marks and paint seams. Waiting was the punishment.

No one raised their voice. No one needed to. Control was built into the routine. Meals arrived at scheduled times. Movement was limited. Conversations were brief and functional. I learned quickly that asking questions only prolonged the silence that followed.

I remember the sound of doors more than anything else. The way they closed with finality, not violence. The click that told my body, before my mind caught up, that I was not free to leave. My body reacted in ways I didn't recognize at first. My stomach stayed tight. Sleep came in fragments. I started counting things without realizing it — steps, tiles, breaths — anything to create structure where there was none.

The lack of information was its own kind of pressure. I didn't know what was happening next. I didn't know how long this would last. I didn't know what decisions were being made about me while I sat waiting.

The uncertainty worked its way into everything.

I became hyper-aware of my movements. How fast I stood. Where my hands rested. How my face looked when someone entered the room. Every interaction felt evaluative, even when no one said a word.

At nineteen, I had never experienced this level of control. I had never understood how completely autonomy could be removed without physical force. The system didn't need to restrain me. It only needed to dictate time and space. Confinement teaches you quickly what matters to those in power.

Not understanding.
Not context.
Compliance.

The days blurred together, marked only by routine and silence. I stopped trying to anticipate outcomes and focused instead on getting through the next hour. The next instruction. The next closed door. I remember thinking that if I could just hold myself together long enough, someone would eventually notice the mistake. That clarity would arrive. That fairness would assert itself.

That belief eroded slowly. Confinement doesn't just restrict your body. It narrows your expectations. By the time I was released from that space, I had learned a lesson I would carry long after: when a system decides you are a problem, waiting becomes a way of breaking you down without ever leaving a mark.

CHAPTER 10

Labeled

The label came before the explanation. It arrived already formed, already approved, already written in language that left no room for objection. By the time I was allowed to see it, the decision had hardened into fact. I remember staring at the word, trying to understand how something so small could carry so much weight. How a few lines of text could undo years of effort, obedience, and belief.

No one asked me if it was accurate.
No one asked me if it was fair.

They spoke about it as if it were inevitable. The room was quiet in the way offices get quiet when empathy has been removed. Fluorescent lights buzzed overhead. Papers were shuffled. Pens clicked. The tone was neutral, almost bored, as if the outcome had already lost its novelty.

This was just another file.

Anger rose before I could stop it—not loud, not explosive, but sharp and focused. A heat in my chest that surprised me with its clarity. I wasn't angry because I didn't understand what was happening. I was angry because I did. I could see how easily the narrative had been inverted. How moments without witnesses had been translated into certainty. How silence had been interpreted as confirmation rather than constraint.

The label did not describe what I had done.
It described how the system now chose to see me.

Disbelief followed quickly behind the anger. Not shock, but a hollow realization that nothing I said at this point would change the outcome. The process had moved too far forward. The language had already done its work.

I remember speaking anyway. Carefully. Calmly. I chose my words as if they might still matter, as if reason could reach through the layers of procedure and find a human being on the other side. The response was procedural.

I was told the decision had been made based on the information available. I was told the system had followed protocol. I was told there were options, appeals, steps—spoken in a way that made it clear none of them were expected to succeed. Coldness settled in then.

Not cruelty. Not hostility.

Something worse. Indifference.

I realized that the people across from me did not need to believe the label was true. They only needed to believe it was sufficient. Sufficient to close the case. Sufficient to move forward. Sufficient to justify what would come next.

At nineteen, I had believed that truth carried weight on its own.

That belief did not survive the labeling.

Once the word was assigned, everything about me shifted. My presence was no longer neutral. My actions were filtered through suspicion. My past was reinterpreted. My future narrowed. The label followed me out of the room.

It attached itself to my name in systems I would never see. It traveled ahead of me, introducing me before I could speak. It explained me away in spaces where I was not allowed to enter. I felt anger again then—deeper, steadier. Not just at what was happening to me, but at how easily it was happening. How smoothly the machine absorbed my life and returned a classification.

The coldest part was this: no one appeared to feel responsible. The label belonged to the system. The consequences belonged to me. That was when I understood that this was no longer about resolution or fairness. It was about containment. About preserving the appearance of order at the expense of truth.

I walked out carrying something invisible but permanent.

And I knew—without being told—that nothing would ever be the same.

CHAPTER 11

Disappeared While Alive

Disappearing didn't happen all at once. It happened in pieces. My access changed first. Places I had moved through freely now required permission or explanation. Conversations shortened. Invitations stopped. I noticed how often my name no longer appeared on lists where it once had.

No one announced that I was being removed.
They simply stopped including me.

Grief came in unexpectedly. Not loud or dramatic, but sudden and disorienting. I grieved the version of myself that had believed effort would be enough. I grieved the future I had imagined—the one built on service, structure, and belonging.

That future collapsed quietly, without ceremony.

I watched it happen from the inside, aware enough to recognize what I was losing but powerless to stop it. Every day brought another small subtraction. Another signal that I no longer fit where I once had. Numbness followed.

It wrapped around me like insulation. Feelings dulled. Time flattened. I stopped expecting clarity or fairness and focused instead on endurance. If I stayed emotionally neutral, I could get through each day without unraveling.

That numbness was not a weakness.
It was protection.

I remember moments when I caught my reflection and barely recognized myself. My posture had changed. My eyes stayed alert even when I was exhausted. I had learned how to exist without drawing attention, how to move through spaces without leaving an imprint.

This is what erasure looks like when it's administrative.

I was still present. Still breathing. Still complying with every requirement placed in front of me. But my voice carried less weight. My explanations were unnecessary. The decisions had already been made. I began to understand that disappearance did not require removal from the building. It only required removal from consideration.

And still, something steadier began to form beneath the numbness.

Resolve.

It was quiet at first. A refusal to fully internalize the narrative being imposed on me. A decision—unspoken, barely conscious—that whatever the system claimed, it would not define the entirety of who I was. I did not yet know how I would reclaim myself. I only knew that I would.

At nineteen, I had been absorbed into a machine that no longer needed me. But I was still here. Still observing. Still remembering. That mattered more than I understood at the time. Because disappearing while alive teaches you something essential: if your existence can be erased on paper, then reclaiming yourself begins somewhere deeper than documentation.

It begins with refusing to vanish inside your own body.

CHAPTER 12

Released but Not Free

Release came with paperwork. Not relief. Not resolution. Paper. I was told where to stand and what to sign, the process unfolding with the same efficiency that had governed everything else. The language suggested closure, as if what had happened could be neatly concluded by completing a checklist.

When I stepped outside, the air felt different. Lighter, maybe. Or maybe I had just grown accustomed to confinement and didn't yet know how to breathe without it. I was no longer being watched in the same way. No one followed my movements. No one told me when to sit or where to go. On the surface, I was free.

And yet, nothing had been returned.

The label came with me. The assumptions came with me. The consequences came with me. I learned quickly that release did not mean restoration. It meant transfer. Control shifted from one system to another, from overt authority to quiet barriers that appeared everywhere I turned.

Applications stalled. Questions were asked and never followed up on. Conversations changed tone once my record entered the room. I could feel it—how interest cooled, how expectations recalibrated.

I wasn't being rejected outright.

I was being filtered.

People didn't accuse me of anything. They didn't need to. The label did that work for them. It hovered in the background, shaping outcomes without explanation.

I began to anticipate it. To brace myself for the moment when doors would close politely instead of slamming. When opportunities would dissolve without reason. When I would be thanked for my time and sent on my way.

That was when anger returned—older now, steadier, sharpened by clarity.

I understood then that the system did not need to keep me confined to control my future. It only needed to mark me. Once marked, others would do the rest. Grief resurfaced too, layered differently this time. Not just for what had been taken, but for what could no longer be reclaimed. The version of myself that trusted systems implicitly. The belief that fairness was automatic.

I carried those losses quietly. There was no space to name them. No process for repair. Release assumed closure. The institution had moved on.

I had not.

At nineteen, I entered believing service would protect me. I exited understanding that protection was conditional—and easily withdrawn. The realization settled heavily, reshaping how I moved through the world. I became careful. Watchful. Skeptical of promises that relied on procedure rather than people. I learned to read fine print the way I once read faces—looking for what wasn't being said.

Still, I survived.

That survival wasn't celebrated. It didn't come with recognition or redemption. It came quietly, through persistence. Through showing up even when I was tired of being explained away.

Released but not free is a strange place to live. Your body moves forward, but part of you remains braced for restraint. You learn to exist in between—outside the walls, yet never fully unmarked. Freedom, I would later learn, is not the absence of confinement.

It is the reclamation of self after the system has decided who you are.

CHAPTER 13

The Aftermath

The aftermath did not arrive with a single moment of reckoning. It unfolded slowly, layering itself into my body, my relationships, and my faith in ways I did not immediately recognize as connected. At first, the changes felt incidental. Fatigue that lingered longer than it should have. Tension that was never fully released. A constant low-level alertness that followed me into places that were supposed to be safe.

My body carried the story even when I tried not to.

Sleep became unreliable. Rest came without restoration. I learned to function while exhausted, to push through discomfort because stopping felt dangerous. Medical appointments continued, but the focus remained surface-level. Symptoms were noted. Causes were not explored. I had learned by then not to volunteer too much. Experience had taught me that explanation did not always lead to care.

Relationships shifted too.

Some people pulled away quietly, unsure how to engage with what I could not easily summarize. Others stayed, but our conversations changed. I noticed how often I edited myself—how quickly I redirected topics, how carefully I chose what to share.

Trust became selective.

I wanted connection, but I also wanted control over how much of myself was visible. Vulnerability felt risky in a world that had already decided what my silence meant. There were moments when I felt profoundly alone, even in rooms full of people. Moments when I realized that what I had been through did not fit neatly into casual conversation or polite concern.

And then there was faith.

Faith did not leave me, but it changed shape.

I stopped expecting it to make things make sense. I stopped asking it to justify what had happened or explain why protection had failed. Instead, faith became a place of refuge—quiet, private, unexamined by anyone else. God was the only witness I trusted.

I prayed differently then. Not with grand requests or rehearsed language, but with fragments. With exhaustion. With honesty that did not need to be defended. Faith became less about answers and more about endurance.

There were days when anger surfaced again—directed not just at institutions, but at the spiritual frameworks that had taught me obedience without equipping me to recognize harm. I wrestled with what it meant to honor authority without surrendering myself to it.

That wrestling mattered.

Over time, I began to see how deeply the experience had shaped me. How it had sharpened my awareness, narrowed my tolerance for ambiguity, and recalibrated my understanding of safety. I was not broken, but I was altered. The aftermath was not a single consequence. It was a constellation.

Health, relationships, and faith did not suffer independently—they informed one another. Exhaustion made connection harder. Isolation intensified physical symptoms. Faith steadied me when nothing else did. Slowly, something else emerged beneath the weight of it all.

Clarity.

I began to recognize patterns—not just in my own experience, but in the stories of others who had been quietly carrying similar aftermaths. Different details. Same structure. Same silence. That recognition planted a question I could not ignore: *What happens when harm is absorbed rather than addressed?* The answer was all around me.

The aftermath is where systems assume the story ends. But for survivors, it is often where the real work begins—learning how to live in a body that remembers, in relationships that require negotiation, and in a faith that has been refined by truth rather than comfort. I was no longer just surviving what had happened.

I was beginning to understand it.

CHAPTER 14

Bearing Witness

For a long time, I believed that surviving was enough. That if I kept moving forward, kept functioning, kept building a life beyond what had happened, the past would eventually lose its hold. I believed silence was a form of control—that by not speaking, I could keep the story contained.

What I didn't realize was that silence was still doing work.

It shaped how I moved through the world. How I measured risk. How I understood authority. Even when I wasn't consciously thinking about the past, it was present—in my body, in my caution, in the way I listened for what wasn't being said. Bearing witness didn't begin with writing. It began with noticing.

I noticed how often similar stories surfaced in quiet conversations. How survivors spoke in fragments, testing whether it was safe to continue. How paperwork was invoked as the final word, even when it contradicted lived reality. Different details. Same structure.

I noticed how easily institutions dismissed harm once it had been administratively resolved. How outcomes were treated as evidence of fairness rather than efficiency. How silence was mistaken for closure. That realization unsettled me more than the original experience. Because it meant this wasn't just about me.

Bearing witness, I learned, is not about accusation. It's about refusal—refusal to allow incomplete records to stand unchallenged as truth. Refusal to let harm remain invisible simply because it was processed correctly. For a long time, I hesitated. Speaking carried risk. Exposure. The possibility of being misunderstood all over again. I knew what it felt like to have my experience reframed by others.

But silence carried risk too.

It allowed the pattern to continue unexamined. It left younger people unprepared. It reinforced the idea that survival required disappearance. I didn't want that legacy.

When I finally began to write, I did so carefully. Not to relive what had happened, but to document it. To anchor memory in language that could not be easily dismissed. To tell the story in a way that honored both truth and restraint. Bearing witness required discipline.

It meant resisting the urge to sensationalize. It meant grounding emotion in clarity. It meant understanding that credibility is not granted by institutions—it is built through consistency and care.

As I wrote, something shifted. The weight I had been carrying redistributed itself. The story no longer lived solely inside my body. It existed outside of me, in words that could be read, examined, and held.

That mattered.

Bearing witness did not erase the past. It did not heal everything. But it did something essential: it broke the isolation. For the first time, I understood that my voice did not need permission to exist. That testimony was not an act of defiance, but an act of integrity.

This book is the result of that understanding.

Not a demand.
Not an accusation.

A record.

CHAPTER 15

Survival Is Not Guilt

Survival has a way of being misinterpreted. It is often mistaken for agreement.For acceptance.
For complicity. I learned early how easily silence could be framed as consent and endurance reframed as responsibility. When harm is processed efficiently, the burden of meaning is quietly shifted onto the person who lived it.

That is not justice.

Justice does not ask survivors to carry what institutions refuse to examine. It does not require pain to be proven through spectacle, nor does it confuse procedural closure with truth. Survival is not guilt. It is evidence.

Evidence of adaptation. Of endurance. Of a body and mind doing what was necessary to remain intact in conditions that did not prioritize care. The fact that I continued—quietly, imperfectly, without permission—does not validate what happened. It exposes it.

Justice, I have learned, is not the same as punishment. It is accountability with memory. It is the willingness to look directly at outcomes and ask how they were produced. It is the refusal to let efficiency replace ethics.

For a long time, I believed justice would arrive as a correction—an acknowledgment, an apology, a reversal. I waited for the system to recognize its own failure. That recognition did not come. What came instead was understanding. Understanding that justice does not always arrive from above. Sometimes it begins at eye level, when survivors name what happened without distortion and refuse to carry blame that does not belong to them.

This book is part of that refusal.

I do not claim perfection in how I navigated what happened. Nineteen-year-olds are not meant to navigate power alone. The expectation that I should have known more, resisted better, spoken sooner—those expectations ignore the conditions under which decisions were made.

Justice accounts for context.
Justice names imbalance.
Justice recognizes that consent cannot exist where safety is absent.

If there is responsibility to be claimed, it belongs where power resided—not where survival occurred.

I have come to understand that telling the truth is not an act of aggression. It is an act of restoration. It restores coherence where there was fragmentation. It restores dignity where there was erasure. It restores the possibility where silence once stood in for peace.

Survival did not absolve the system.
It revealed it.

I am no longer interested in being explained away by records that were never designed to hold the full story. I am interested in clarity—in ensuring that what happened is understood accurately, even if it is uncomfortable. Justice does not require cruelty. It requires courage.

Courage to listen without defensiveness.
Courage to examine process, not just outcome.
Courage to believe survivors without demanding they disappear afterward.

I survived. That fact stands independent of anyone's approval. And because I survived, I speak—not to accuse, but to bear witness; not to punish, but to insist that truth be allowed to stand where silence once did the work of denial.

This is not the end of my story. It is the end of my captivity.

Afterword

To the Survivor Who Reads This

You matter.

You are not alone.

You are not what they did to you.

You are not crazy.

You are not to blame.

You are not broken.

You are not weak.

You are holy.

You are loved.

APPENDIX: RESOURCES FOR MST SURVIVORS & VETERANS (U.S.)

1. VA RESOURCES — MST & HEALTHCARE SUPPORT

Veterans Affairs (VA) Military Sexual Trauma (MST) Services

- The VA provides free mental health and medical care related to MST, regardless of disability status or documentation of the event.

- MST treatment options include outpatient counseling, residential care, and evidence-based therapies such as prolonged exposure (PE), cognitive processing therapy, and EMDR.

MST Coordinator at VA Medical Centers

Every VA facility has a designated MST Coordinator to help survivors find local treatment, care options, and referrals.

Beyond MST (Free Mobile App)

A secure self-help app with tools for coping and managing MST effects.

Vet Center Counseling

Community-based counseling for transitions, trauma recovery, and MST support available through local Vet Centers.

VA Crisis Resources (24/7)

- National Suicide & Crisis Lifeline: Call or text 988
- National Call Center for Homeless Veterans: 877-424-3838 (TTY: 711) — 24/7 support and housing referrals.

Make the Connection

A VA-supported platform with veteran videos and recovery resources, including MST stories.

2. **NONPROFIT ORGANIZATIONS & SUPPORT NETWORKS**

Code of Support Foundation

Provides casework assistance, peer networking, and outreach for veterans and families navigating complex systems.

GI Rights Network (Hotline: 877-447-4487)

Free, confidential counseling on military discharge questions and veteran rights; connects veterans with supportive services.

Swords to Plowshares

Veterans service organization that helps with job training, housing support, benefits advocacy, and holistic case management.

Warrior Care Network

Offers no-cost intensive outpatient mental health services — including PTSD and MST-inclusive care — through partnerships with academic medical centers.

1in6

Supports male survivors of sexual abuse, including MST survivors; offers online support groups and helpline options.

Military OneSource — MST Support

Information about MST, related treatment options, and referrals to non-medical support resources.

3. **HOUSING & HOMELESS PREVENTION RESOURCES**

National Call Center for Homeless Veterans — 877-424-3838

24/7 access to the crisis line with housing referrals and local homeless programs.

VA Homeless Programs (HCHV & HUD-VASH)

- **Health Care for Homeless Veterans (HCHV)**: Outreach, case management, and residential treatment referrals.

- HUD-VASH: Long-term rental assistance vouchers with case management.

Supportive Services for Veteran Families (SSVF)

Provides eviction prevention, rapid re-housing funds, security deposit assistance, and case management.

Grant and Per Diem (GPD) Programs

Transitional housing resources; some offer women-only or family-friendly placements.

LifeSTEPS (Women Veteran Support)

Nonprofit focused on trauma-informed housing support and stability plans for women veterans, including mothers, with individualized plans.

4. TRANSITION, JOB TRAINING & EMPLOYMENT

National Resource Directory (NRD)

A government portal that links service members, veterans, and caregivers with thousands of resources for employment, education, housing, and health services.

Swords to Plowshares Employment & Training

Veteran-focused job training services and employer connections to support career placement.

VA Vocational Rehabilitation & Employment (VR&E)

Provides employment services, career counseling, and training for veterans with service-connected conditions (contact your local VA). *(implied as widely available VA support)*

Department of Labor — Homeless Veterans' Reintegration Program (HVRP)

Career training and employment support for veterans, including women and veterans with families *(often stateside/local resource networks)*

5. **WOMEN VETERAN–SPECIFIC & FAMILY SUPPORT**

Center for Women Veterans (VA)

Coordinates VA healthcare, benefits, and services specifically for women veterans.

Women Veterans Health Program

Comprehensive women's health and reproductive services through VA facilities.

Support for Women with Children

Family-friendly transitional housing, childcare grant referrals, and women-focused case management through HUD-VASH and GPD programs with bridge housing options.

National Domestic Violence Hotline

24/7 support for survivors of intimate partner violence; not VA-specific but helpful for MST survivors navigating safety concerns: 1-800-799-SAFE (7233) *(implied national resource)*

6. **MENTAL HEALTH & CRISIS SUPPORT**

VA MST Treatment Resources

Free MST-specific counseling, group therapy, and peer support across VA medical centers and clinics.

Beyond MST App

Free app with tools to cope with emotional and psychological effects of military sexual trauma.

VA Mental Health Services

Access care through local VA providers, referrals from an MST coordinator, or by calling the VA mental health hotline.

Make the Connection

Online videos and recovery community stories that share lived experiences and coping strategies.

7. **LEGAL & RIGHTS SUPPORT**

GI Rights Network Hotline — 877-447-4487

Free counseling on discharge issues, veterans' rights, options, and referrals.

Veterans Service Organizations (VSOs)

Organizations like Disabled American Veterans (DAV), American Legion, Veterans of Foreign Wars (VFW), Wounded Warrior Project (Post 9/11), and County VSO can help file VA claims, appeal denials, and navigate benefits through accredited representatives. *(common VSO support)*

HOW TO USE THIS LIST

✔ Call a centralized number (like the Homeless Veterans Center or MST coordinator) first.

✔ If you're struggling with housing, call the National Call Center for Homeless Veterans (877-424-3838).

✔ If you're seeking mental health support specifically for MST, reach out to your VA MST Coordinator or a local Vet Center.

✔ You don't need a service connection to receive MST-related care.

A NOTE TO SURVIVORS

If you are reading this while struggling:

- You are not alone.
- You are not imagining what happened.
- Help exists, even if the system makes it hard to find.

This book is not a substitute for care—but it is proof that survival is possible.

ADDITIONAL HEALING RESOURCES BY THE AUTHOR

The following books and journals are offered as optional tools for grounding, reflection, and spiritual healing. They are not substitutes for medical or mental health care, but may be supportive companions for survivors navigating trauma recovery, faith, and self-reclamation.

Divine Awakening Manifestation Journal

by Aliya Fitz El

Available on Amazon

This guided manifestation journal is designed to help readers reconnect with their inner voice, clarify intentions, and envision a life beyond survival. Through daily visualization prompts, reflective exercises, and intentional writing practices, this journal supports grounding, hope-building, and future-focused healing.

This resource may be helpful for survivors who:

- Feel disconnected from purpose after trauma

- Are rebuilding identity after institutional harm

- Want a structured, gentle way to reimagine safety and possibility

Survival & Strength: A 60-Day Healing Journal for Survivors

by Aliya Fitz El

Available on Amazon

Created specifically with trauma survivors in mind, this journal offers daily prompts, grounding practices, creative expression exercises, and soul-anchoring Bible verses. It is designed to meet survivors where they are—without pressure to "move on" or minimize pain.

This journal may be helpful for survivors who:

- Are navigating military sexual trauma or complex trauma
- Need grounding tools during periods of emotional distress
- Want faith-anchored reflection without judgment or forced positivity

A Note from the Author

These works were created from lived experience—not theory.

They exist because survival does not end when the trauma stops, and healing does not follow a straight line.

Use what helps. Leave what does not.

You are allowed to heal at your own pace.

Author's Closing Note

I wrote *Captive* with God's hand steadying mine.

Not because faith erased what happened—but because faith kept me alive long enough to tell the truth.

I entered the Marine Corps believing in honor, structure, and service. I also believed, as I was taught, that God walks with those who walk uprightly. What I did not understand then was how often institutions invoke God while ignoring His commands to protect the vulnerable, defend the innocent, and act justly.

This book is not written in anger.

It is written in obedience.

Obedience to truth.

Obedience to conscience.

Obedience to the quiet but unrelenting call to stop carrying what was never meant to be borne alone.

Scripture tells us that what is hidden will be brought into the light. That light is not punishment—it is clarity. And clarity is necessary for healing, repentance, and change.

What happened to me was not God's will.

What followed—my survival, my voice, my refusal to disappear—was God's provision.

To the survivor reading this: you are not forsaken. God was not absent in your suffering, even if the people who claimed authority were. Your body learned how to survive because it had to. There is no shame in that.

To those in leadership: faith without accountability is hollow. Silence in the face of harm is not loyalty—it is failure.

I release this story now, not to condemn, but to testify. Not to seek vengeance, but to insist on truth. Not to remain captive, but to walk free.

God is not afraid of the truth. And neither am I.

— Aliya Fitz El

ABOUT THE AUTHOR

Aliya Fitz El is a United States Marine Corps veteran, author, minister, and advocate for survivors of military sexual trauma and institutional abuse.

She entered the Marine Corps in 2001, following in the footsteps of her father and grandfather, and quickly distinguished herself through discipline, leadership, and performance. Her service was marked by early promotion and dedication—until she reported mistreatment and experienced retaliation, confinement, and wrongful separation.

Aliya is a survivor of military sexual trauma and systemic retaliation. Her work centers truth-telling, accountability, and healing for survivors navigating military and federal systems. She writes from lived experience, faith, and moral conviction—refusing silence where injustice persists.

In addition to *Captive* and *Enslaved*, Aliya is the author of guided healing journals focused on grounding, faith, and post-trauma restoration. She is the founder of Divine Essence Healing Ministry, where she supports survivors through spiritual care, advocacy, and community-based healing.

Aliya continues to speak, write, and advocate for those whose voices were suppressed.

www.ingramcontent.com/pod-product-compliance
Lightning Source LLC
LaVergne TN
LVHW090536110826
845146LV00003B/1120

* 9 7 9 8 9 9 5 4 9 5 1 0 9 *